CW00404870

TABBY LAMB

Tabby Lamb is a non-l
performer based in East London. Equally
inspired by Carly Rae Jepsen and
Tennessee Williams, she strives to tell
stories that explore the intersections
between popular culture and politics.

Their debut solo show *Since U Been Gone*,
which Tabby wrote and performed,
premiered at the Edinburgh Festival
Fringe in 2019, after previewing at the
Gate Theatre, London. The show was
spectacularly received by audiences and
garnered a glowing four-star review from
the *Guardian* who called the play 'bold,
honest and swollen with love'.

Tabby is the Sky Arts Artistic Associate at
Theatre Royal Stratford East, Associate
Writer with Middle Child, and is on
attachment at both Oxford Playhouse and
Royal & Derngate, Northampton. Current
commissions include work for Royal &
Derngate, Middle Child and Proteus.

Alongside their passion for writing, Tabby
is an activist and facilitator who runs
creative arts projects for the LGBTQ+
community. She is developing various
stage and TV projects including a new
Trans musical. You can find her rambles
on Twitter @thetabbylamb and her thirst
traps on Instagram @badgalenby.

Tabby Lamb

HAPPY MEAL

Or the Trans Internet Play

NICK HERN BOOKS
London
www.nickhernbooks.co.uk

A Nick Hern Book

Happy Meal first published in Great Britain as a paperback original in 2022 by Nick Hern Books Limited, The Glasshouse, 49a Goldhawk Road, London W12 8QP, in association with Roots and Theatre Royal Plymouth

Happy Meal copyright © 2022 Tabby Lamb

Tabby Lamb has asserted her right to be identified as the author of this work

Cover photography by Michael Wharley; design by Rebecca Pitt

Designed and typeset by Nick Hern Books, London
Printed in Great Britain by Mimeo Ltd, Huntingdon, Cambridgeshire PE29 6XX

A CIP catalogue record for this book is available from the British Library

ISBN 978 1 83904 108 2

Happy Meal was a Roots and Theatre Royal Plymouth co-production in association with ETT and Oxford Playhouse. It was first performed at the Traverse Theatre, Edinburgh, as part of the 2022 Edinburgh Festival Fringe, on 4 August 2022, before touring. The cast was as follows:

ALEX	Sam Crerar (they/he)
BETTE	Allie Daniel (she/her)
Writer	Tabby Lamb (they/she)
Director	Jamie Fletcher (she/her)
Set and Costume	Ben Stones (he/him)
Video	Daniel Denton (he/him)
Lighting	Kieron Johnson (they/them)
Sound	Eliyana Evans (she/her)
Dramaturg	Jennifer Bakst (she/her)
Deputy Stage Manager	Cat Simpson (she/her)
Producer for Roots	Steven Atkinson (he/him)
Production Manager	Tom Robbins (he/him)
Head of Production for Theatre Royal Plymouth	Hugh Borthwick (he/him)
Marketing	Emma Martin (she/her)
Press	Michelle Manghan (she/her)

Sets and properties built by Theatre Royal Plymouth

Roots is a queer Yorkshire touring theatre company that creates new productions through ambitious collaborations between citizens and artists. Based in Tadcaster and resident at York Theatre Royal, *Happy Meal* is Roots' first touring production from its slate of projects in development with queer artists.

Happy Meal by Tabby Lamb is a Roots commission.

4-6 Bridge Street, Tadcaster, North Yorkshire, LS24 9AL
www.rootstouring.com | 07568 585841

Roots' work is possible thanks to the generous donations of: Arts Council England, Backstage Trust, The Martin Bowley Charitable Trust, National Lottery Community Fund, Foyle Foundation, City of York Council, Old Possum's Practical Trust.

Theatre
Royal
Plymouth

Theatre Royal Plymouth is a registered charity providing art, education and community engagement throughout Plymouth and the wider region. We engage and inspire many communities through performing arts and we aim to touch the lives and interests of people from all backgrounds. We do this by creating and presenting a breadth of shows on a range of scales, with our extensive creative engagement programmes, by embracing the vitality of new talent and supporting emerging and established artists, and by collaborating with a range of partners to provide dynamic cultural leadership for the city of Plymouth.

Recent productions and co-productions include *Delicate* (with Extraordinary Bodies and Nordland Visual Theatre), *Happy Meal* by Tabby Lamb (with Roots), *Today I Killed My Very First Bird* (with Voodoo Monkeys), *Sorry, You're Not A Winner* by Samuel Bailey (with Paines Plough), *MUM* by Morgan Lloyd Malcolm (with Francesca Moody Productions and Soho Theatre, in association with Popcorn Group), *NHS The Musical* by Nick Stimson and Jimmy Jewell, *Amsterdam* by Maya Arad Yasur (with Actors Touring Company and Orange Tree

Theatre), *I Think We Are Alone* by Sally Abbott (with Frantic Assembly), *The Strange Tale of Charlie Chaplin and Stan Laurel* (with Told By An Idiot), *One Under* by Winsome Pinnock (with Graeae), *The Unreturning* by Anna Jordan (with Frantic Assembly) and *You Stupid Darkness!* by Sam Steiner (with Paines Plough).

Theatre Royal Plymouth specialises in the production of new plays alongside the presentation of a broad range of theatre – including classic and contemporary drama, musicals, opera, ballet and dance. We have three performance spaces – The Lyric, The Drum and The Lab. TRP has a strong track record of presenting and producing international work from companies and artists including Ontroerend Goed, Big In Belgium at the Edinburgh Festival Fringe, Robert Lepage and the late Yukio Ninagawa. In March 2019, TRP unveiled *Messenger*, the UK's largest lost wax bronze sculpture created by the artist Joseph Hillier.

HAPPY MEAL

Author's Note
Tabby Lamb

This play was inspired by three people.
Number One is my dear friend Nicol who
once turned to me and said, 'You were
born in exactly the right body.' This
sentence is what prompted me to begin
creating a world where lines like this are
normal.

Number Two is my fiancé, my very own
Alec, who every single day inspires me to
be the very best version of me possible –
for myself, for them and for our
community. I've rarely met anyone as
kind or as caring, and I hope one day to
be as good a person as they are.

Number Three is my fiancé's father, who
passed away just before rehearsals
began. Doug created the person I love the
most in the world, embraced his weird
future daughter-in-law, and in fact he was
the very first person to call me 'daughter'.
I learnt so much from him, from the fact
that a single *Star Wars* film is not called a
Star War, to how to be myself at any age,
and how it's never too late to stop

learning and growing. I hope that Alec and Bette continue to learn, grow and develop long after the final line of this play. They deserve to live lives as full of love and happiness as Doug did.

Finally, this play is for every single Trans person who wants to see themselves on stage. It's for future Alecs and Bettes, future audience members, every single one of us who put on *Maid in Manhattan* and said, 'This would be better if JLo had a dick.'

Characters

ALEX, *Trans masc, starts the play as thirteen years old and outwardly identifying as a lesbian, he comes out at sixteen, changes his name and starts T at eighteen*

BETTE, *Trans femme, starts the play at thirteen years old and not out at all*

The characters must be played by actual Trans people.

Note on Staging

This play is set entirely online, but it should be performed live and in person. There are brief moments where the two characters may physically acknowledge each other, but for the most part it must be clear that they are in separate locations and not interacting in the physical sense. The online communications affect the characters' spelling and language choices, as well as the use of abbreviations. These can be pronounced however you decide.

The internet changes and develops as the play goes on, so the representation of the internet should also change. However you and your design team decide to portray the internet, I ask that it is not simply through screens or projections – though I expect either or both will be used as one part of the design concept. This is a play for a reason, and a physical abstract representation of the internet is of utmost importance.

The play should be physically hard to perform at first, with stilted dialogue. The characters will get more used to the performance and more at ease on stage as the play (and the internet) develops, until we are at present day with merely a millisecond pause between people around the world. This technological shift should be represented physically in the staging.

This text went to press before the end of rehearsals and so may differ slightly from the play as performed.

Preshow

We are in a cartoon teenage dream of the Arctic – there are igloos, a hockey rink, a yellow school bus and even a pizza parlour. Maybe all these locations are on stage already – or maybe as the characters move around in the preshow they discover these new places.

We see a leaderboard, BETTE's *screen name is highlighted at Number Three with 380,000,000 coins. As the audience enters,* BETTE's *penguin has a pink beanie with cat ears on, and some pink high-top trainers and/or more cool accessories.* BETTE *is playing different games in the world to gain 'coins'. Maybe we see her fishing, and earning coins for each fish, maybe she's scoring goals in ice hockey, gaining more coins. For each coin she earns, the leaderboard updates.*

The house lights go down when ALEX *logs in. We hear him arrive and see him appear at the bottom of the leaderboard with 00 coins. His penguin is very basic – no accessories at all.*

Scene One

Club Penguin – 2003

A 'Challenge' pop-up appears in front of ALEX, he must choose 'Accept' or 'Reject'.

He accepts.

ALEX *and* BETTE *put on jetpacks and their penguin avatars fly through the sky in a race to collect the most coins (and be first to the finish line).*

It's neck-and-neck.

Then ALEX *is ahead.*

Then BETTE *gets more coins.*

Then ALEX *hits a jackpot coin and multiple coins rain down.*

Then BETTE *overtakes – but* ALEX *grabs her leg and is pulled along with her – she shakes herself free by throwing coins at him.*

They are neck-and-neck.

BETTE *wins by a millisecond?*

Stars and coins and snowflakes rain down as a winner banner is unfurled above BETTE.

The leaderboard is updated and now BETTE *is Number One! As* BETTE *and* ALEX *talk, speech bubbles pop up over them.*

BETTE. Don't hate the player.

ALEX. Well I don't hate the game.

BETTE. Why are you being such a d*ck?

ALEX. I'm not being a d*ck? I'm playing... this is a game y'know?

BETTE. It's technically an Arctic-themed open-world simulation that builds social skills alongside helping to teach things like internet safety, basic maths and even hand–eye coordination.

Beat.

Or that's how I convince my mum to let me stay on here so long anyway.

ALEX. Damn girl, you got this all figured out don't you?

ALEX *thinks* BETTE *is a girl.* BETTE *doesn't even think she's a girl yet – but she doesn't correct him. She likes it.*

BETTE. What can I say, you don't get to be the UK under-sixteen Penguin of the

Month five months in a row without being a f*cking icon.

ALEX. Do icons usually have cat ears?

BETTE. They do here – cost me nine thousand coins, these did, limited-edition Xtina collection I'll have you know. You could afford something *slightly less iconic* now.

ALEX. I can?

BETTE. I mean I beat you fair and square, but you still get coins for second place – plus some of those dodgy moves you pulled got you some of my winnings I think? I don't normally do the multiplayer games, I'm a bit of a hermit penguin.

ALEX. Ooh a Solitary Man eh?

BETTE. I couldn't quite say that.

ALEX. Solitary woMan maybe?

BETTE. And a Neil Diamond reference? Wow. How old are you?!

ALEX. Neil Diamond? Who do you think I am? I'm clearly talking about the iconic HIM cover.

BETTE. Him?

ALEX. HIM – His Infernal Majesty, they're a Finnish band with the fittest lead singer ever.

BETTE. Finnish?!

ALEX. Yeah, check them out – they're
pretty cool, and Ville Valo is just...
dreamy. I won a competition on Kerrang
One-oh-five-point-two to meet them,
but I couldn't go. Fuming.

BETTE. I'll check them out.

ALEX. And listen, I didn't know about the
coins – I haven't been here before.
I wasn't trying to steal from you – I just
didn't know what to do so...

BETTE. It's okay, I needed a bit of a fire
under my butt anyway, was getting a bit
complacent always being on the top of
the leaderboard *worldwide*, I should've
guessed you were new here anyway,
I mean your avi is so pov.

ALEX. A classist penguin – now I've seen
everything.

BETTE. Everything except the top of the
worldwide leaderboard.

ALEX. Oh that'll change – just you wait.

BETTE. I could teach you, but I'd have to
charge.

ALEX. Your penguin brings all the boys to
the yard and they're like 'You're better
than me'.

BETTE. Damn right I'm better than you.

Glad to hear you know some music in the English language too.

ALEX. I mean, everyone knows 'Milkshake' don't they? Incubus covered it on their last tour for f*ck's sake?

Beat.

So, when's my first lesson?

BETTE. Right now! What do you wanna know?

ALEX. Do all the penguins look as gay as yours?

BETTE. No, I'm special. End of lessons. F*ck off.

ALEX. Oh sh*t I didn't mean it in like a bad way – I meant like... are there other clothing options beside pink? And how do I get them?

BETTE. 'Didn't mean it in a bad way.'

Beat.

ALEX *throws a snowball at himself, coins appear. Beat.*

He does it again, and again, until he has no coins left.

You didn't have to...

BETTE *claims the coins.*

Let's go get you some new clothes.

BETTE *takes* ALEX *towards the Penguin Parlour.*

Scene Two

Myspace – 2004

We see BETTE *scrolling Myspace, trying to find* ALEX. *She finds him, and begins to scroll through his page – but it keeps changing.*

We then see two Myspace pages next to each other, they are being updated. We see old text being deleted and new text being written. We see spelling mistakes being made, we see rewrites and edits to new text. We see background images and colours changing, new songs being selected and uploaded.

We might see just the updates, or we might see the coding that goes into them too.

Throughout the updates, we also see ALEX *taking multiple selfies from the*

'Myspace angle'. Some with his hair in an emo fringe, some in a beanie, some in a snapback – all trying to appear as masc as possible. When we see these photos, they should be images of Trans kids the real age of the character – not the adults playing them.

ALEX's profile details:

Name: Al.

Profile URL: Myspace.com/thexsunxisxsettingxonxme

Last Log In: 21 February.

About Me Before Edits: Im 14, in year 9 @ Caldies. Top set 4everyfing (LOL JK) Um... I like music?

BETTE. 'Um... I like music'.

About Me After Edits: Al, 14, cool.

Cool – much better.

ALEX's interests:

General: Um, I play guitar? I watch The Simpsons and Family Guy?

Family Guy?

I hope your music taste is better than your TV taste.

ALEX. Music: A Static Lullaby, AFI, Alkaline Trio, American Hi-Fi, All-American

Rejects, The Ataris, Blink 182, Brand New, Coheed and Cambria, Dashboard Confessional, Fall Out Boy, Funeral for a Friend, Green Day, Good Charlotte, HIM, Hellogoodbye, Jimmy Eat World, Less Than Jake, Linkin Park, Motion City Soundtrack, My Chemical Romance, New Found Glory, Panic! At The Disco, Simple Plan, Sum 41.

BETTE. Alphabetised? Impressive.

ALEX. Films: Edward Scissorhands, The Matrix, But I'm a Cheerleader, Charlie's Angels, Johnny English, Monsters, Inc., Scary Movie, Tomb Raider, Lord of the Rings and Daredevil.

BETTE's profile details:

Name: BETTEr Luck Next Time.

Profile URL: Myspace.com/xcoldxblackxheartx.

Last Log In: 28 February.

About Me: Bad Ass Biatch.

BETTE's interests: Full-on gamer, currently loving Prince of Persia, Final Fantasy X-2, Tony Hawk, Doom, Spyro, obv Britney's Dance Beat (lol) and Sabrina the Teenage Witch: Potion Commotion.

General: Pretty much just Video Games, The Sims and obviously Neopets.

Music: Britney, Girls Aloud, Pussycat Dolls, Panic! At The Disco, Busted, Jonas Brothers, Blue, S Club 7.

We see BETTE add in Nightwish, Evanescence and HIM to impress ALEX.

ALEX. Evanescence, Nightwish... and HIM eh? Maybe there's hope for you yet...

Films: Camp, High School Musical, House of Wax, Breakfast on Pluto, The Hottie & The Nottie, Camp Rock, The Princess Diaries, Hedwig and the Angry Inch, The Nightmare Before Christmas, Finding Nemo and Bridget Jones's Diary.

ALEX is on Limewire, downloading music – we see albums by bands like Hundred Reasons, Korn, Limp Biscuit, etc. He downloads a file titled simply 'Patrick' and copies it into an email to BETTE.

Some homework for you – listen to this album and lmk if I judged your taste right?

Scene Three

MSN – 2005

ALEX*'s image is Shane from* The L Word, BETTE*'s image is Karen from* Will and Grace. *We watch their chat screen, but maybe also the rest of their internet scrolling as they talk.*

BETTE. You're late.

ALEX. It's Tuesday, you know I'm always late on Tuesdays.

BETTE. Oh yeah – choir practice.

ALEX. HOW MANY TIMES?! It's not choir practice?

BETTE. What were you playing today?

ALEX. 'Give Me Oil in My Lamp'.

BETTE. Sounds pretty Jesusy to me.

ALEX. It'll look good on my UCAS! Anyway I'm here now and we've still got five minutes before it starts.

BETTE. Whatever nerd – Did you read the *Buffy* bit in this week's *Smash Hits*?

ALEX. Of course –

BETTE. I still don't believe she dies, but apparently she hasn't been seen on set since, so maybe she really is...

ALEX. I'm more focused on the kiss, TBH.

BETTE. What is it about two girls kissing that gets straight boys so hot and bothered?!

ALEX. Don't ask me?

BETTE. Well I am asking you – like did you even fancy Willow before or is it just 'cause she's kissing a girl?

ALEX. Come on B, I've seen your Tumblr. 'Emo Boys Kissing' is like your number-one search term.

BETTE. Touché, but seriously – what is it about lesbians?

ALEX *realises they have never discussed gender or sexuality directly.* BETTE *thinks* ALEX *is a cis boy,* ALEX *thinks* BETTE *is a cis girl.*

So...

ALEX. I mean, girls are hot right?

BETTE. I mean, the general consensus does seem to be yes.

ALEX. Oh come on! The way you've spoken about Willow and Anya before... I know you can appreciate a woman.

BETTE. Of course I can! Like, all three of my friends are women (with you being the obvious exception).

ALEX. It's just like watching anyone you fancy making out with someone else you fancy, y'know? It kinda becomes art – like you're not jealous of them, you're not feeling left out, you're just appreciating the aesthetics of two beautiful people enjoying each other's beauty – and yes some boys take it too far, and some boys are gross but like... in its purest form it's pure.

BETTE. So you're not one of those boys?

ALEX. I am not one of *those* boys.

BETTE. Okay, it's about to start – I'm gonna grab some tissues and head downstairs. Chat tomorrow?

ALEX. Chat tomorrow, I'll grab some tissues too. Winky face.

BETTE. Gross.

Scene Four

MSN – 2005

Time passes, we see them both scroll the internet separately. We pick up a week or so later.

BETTE. What U Up 2?

ALEX. Not much really, just finished watching *The Simpsons*.

BETTE. Ah yes, it's gone six p.m. How could I forget.

ALEX. I'm surprised you're even alive after the drama of *Neighbours*.

BETTE. Oh haha – today was actually v. dramatique.

ALEX. Oooh what happened?

BETTE. Someone broke into Lassiters, but we don't know whooooo.

ALEX. Sounds wild (!).

BETTE. You know I'm addicted, don't judge. What U Up 2 this weekend anyway?

ALEX. I'm actually going on a date...

BETTE. Ooh! Where are you gonna take her?

ALEX. Well I was gonna take her to the cinema, but her ex works there so I think we'll go bowling instead?

BETTE. Why would her ex have a problem? Is he giving you both a hard time?

ALEX. It's she actually – and I think she wants them to get back together.

BETTE. So, your date's bisexual?

ALEX. Lol no – she's a proper gold-star lesbian.

BETTE. Wait what?! Why is a lesbian going out with you???

ALEX. 'Cause I'm gay you twat.

BETTE. I mean you are going on a date with a girl apparently, so that doesn't quite track.

ALEX. Oh fuck.

BETTE. Did you only just realise?

ALEX. No I meant like 'oh fuck I didn't think telling you this through did I'.

BETTE. What do you mean?

ALEX. So I am a boy, like – I haven't lied to you or anything... but well, not everyone knows I'm a boy.

BETTE. So you're going on a date with a girl whilst pretending to be a girl? You don't think she's gonna notice? Or have you gone for some real dykey bird who's never been kissed 'n'll be grateful for the attention anyway lol.

ALEX. WTF? First of all don't say dyke second of all wtf 'grateful for the attention'?!

BETTE. Don't change the subject.

ALEX. I'm not changing the subject – I'm pointing out *just one small fraction* of your wild ignorance, which, actually *is* right on subject because I AM NOT PRETENDING TO BE A GIRL.

BETTE. Then what wtf is actually going on rn?

Beat.

Al?

Alex...?

Oh come the fuck on Bridget – just tell me what's happening.

ALEX. I'm Transgender.

Beat.

I'm not out yet.

BETTE. OMG like Nadia from *Big Brother*?! Iconic!

ALEX. You... don't mind?

BETTE. I mean, not really? I don't care if you've got a cock or a fanny TBH.

ALEX. It doesn't really have much to do with my bits – but, thanks.

BETTE. So is that why you got mad at me for saying dyke? 'Cause you wanna be one?

ALEX. I didn't get mad – I just called you out, because it's not your word. It's a word that some lesbians are trying to reclaim after having it hurled at them abusively for like... ages. And I don't want to be a dyke, people IRL already think I am. I'm not 'like Nadia' I'm... the other way, y'know?

BETTE. The other way? Like... a girl who wants to be a boy? I don't think I'm getting this, am I? I'm sorry. I get all of my queer education from *Will and Grace* and fucking *Eurotrash* so I'm not gonna have the right words or the right I dunno... terminology, but I love you right? We're best mates. Whether you're a boy or a girl or Scooby fuckin' Doo. OKAY?

ALEX. I'm more of a Scrappy Doo TBH.

BETTE. You know what I meant.

ALEX. Yeah, I understand and thank you. Gender Performance via Scooby Doo characters is quite good idea though – maybe I'll make a gender theorist out of you yet! Just... watch your language eh? God I sound like my mum.

Message sending failed.

BETTE. So what's she like?

ALEX. Oh FFS – I think Mum unplugged the modem again.

Message sending failed.

BETTE. Is she more of a Buffy or a Cordelia?

ALEX. Her and Dad have been fighting a lot.

Message sending failed.

BETTE. Oh come on don't ignore me Al! I said we were best mates, didn't I?

ALEX. And she always wants to call Auntie Maureen after an argument.

Message sending failed.

BETTE. I can stop asking about her? Why are you being such a prick? I didn't mean to upset you – I'm trying, I really am?

ALEX. Are you getting any of these?

Message sending failed.

BETTE. If you're not gonna talk to me I give up. I'm sorry I'm not your perfect little date.

ALEX's internet reconnects, and all the messages are sent simultaneously – but BETTE has already logged out.

ALEX. Yeah, I understand and thank you. Gender Performance via Scooby Doo characters is quite a good idea though – maybe I'll make a gender theorist out of you yet! Just... watch your language eh? God, I sound like my mum. Oh FFS – I think Mum unplugged the modem again. Her and Dad have been fighting a lot. And she always wants to call Auntie Maureen after an argument. Are you getting any of these?

Oh you've already gone haven't you.

Shit.

Scene Five

Various Corners of the Internet

BETTE *spirals – she thinks* ALEX *ignored her and she dives more into the internet. We see her chatting to other people on MSN, she tries to flirt, badly. We see her opening a porn site, 89.com, and hovering over the gay categories, and also the Trans categories. She changes her Myspace relationship status to 'in a relationship' and then back to 'single' multiple times.*

She takes numerous selfies for new MSN pictures. Trying to look more femme. In some she tries lipstick, we then see her rub it off in disgust, some in a wig – which then flies across the room. We see her looking at a bra but decide not to put it on. Again these images should all portray the age of the character, not the actor. She deletes them all.

She goes to Club Penguin and tops the leaderboard again – she deletes her account. She messages 'Cyber?' to multiple MSN accounts, updates her sexuality on Myspace to 'gay' then back to 'straight' then finally to 'undisclosed'.

She starts an email to ALEX: *'Dear Al...' then deletes it.*

She updates her MSN screen name to Avril Lavigne lyrics (with multiple emojis).

She sees ALEX *online on MSN, and changes her visibility to 'appear offline' then back to 'online'.*

A chat box from ALEX *pops up.*

ALEX. Hiiiiiiiiiiiiiiiiiiiiiiiiiii.

Scene Six

Neopets – 2006

In a forgotten corner of the internet,
ALEX *agrees to meet with* BETTE *to learn
about Neopets – actional online
Tamagotchi-type pets that* BETTE *plays
with frequently. The site was popular in
2003ish, but she never stopped playing.*

BETTE. Welcome to Neopia... land of the
cute, home of the weird! Here you get
to create and adopt your very own pet
without all the hassle of walkies! Our
Neopets come in all sorts of shapes and
sizes, with breeds and accessories to
match even the most unique of
personalities! What brings you here
today, my good man?

ALEX. You did.

BETTE. Oh come on, play along.

ALEX. Oh um... I am here to get a pet?

BETTE. Well, hold your horses there,
cowboy, before you can adopt a pet
you're gonna need a house that fits all
the NPPP Guidelines.

ALEX. The what now?

BETTE. The Neopet Protection Program. Now let's find you the pet sanctuary of your dreams.

ALEX. Do we have to?

BETTE *ignores him.*

BETTE. Neopia Central which is entry-level basic-bitch zone TBH, then there's Faerieland which is gorge and has clouds that actually float across the skyline, I reckon you'd like the Haunted Woods though... Wanna check it out and make a bid? It takes twenty-four hours for the Neocouncil to approve all new residential dwellings so choose carefully.

ALEX. Hours? It was quicker for me to realise I'm queer, come out to my parents, meet my girlfriend, introduce her to my parents, exchange promise rings and break up?

BETTE *starts to pet and feed her Neopet, growing more frustrated with ALEX.*

BETTE. You came out to your parents?!

ALEX. Only halfway – you're still the only one who knows I'm a boy.

BETTE. Not even your... wait YOU BROKE UP?!

ALEX. Oh yeah, it's not a big deal – it was basically like a fifteen-minute thing. We went bowling on Friday and then the Monday after I broke up with her right after maths.

BETTE. Wow.

ALEX. You know me, always on to the next thing.

BETTE. Well patience is a virtue.

ALEX. I'm sorry I didn't tell you – I've been trying to but you're on here all the time now.

Why'd you think I logged in today?
I just... wanted some *us time* again.

I didn't mean anything by it – I forgot I even told you I had a girlfriend if I'm honest?

BETTE. Oh wow some gentleman you're gonna be. She'll always be your first girlfriend now.

ALEX. I hadn't thought about it like that.

BETTE. I can't even imagine my first...

ALEX. I can. Devil face.

BETTE. Not now dude.

ALEX. Sorry.

BETTE. For the smutty joke or for ignoring me for weeks?

ALEX. I have not been ignoring you for weeks! Days maybe... you know what it's like – exam time and Mum breathing down my neck about UCAS already. She never went to uni so she's like KEEN you get me?

BETTE. Must be nice to have a caring mother.

ALEX. Drama queen.

BETTE. Guilty!

Your world just seems so... big.

ALEX. Your world is only as big as you make it – time to start drawing outside the lines maybe?

BETTE. You got a pencil sharpener?

ALEX. Lol.

What are your results-day plans?

BETTE. People make results-day plans?

ALEX. Yeah! Like, the Pashmina Girls at my school are throwing some big picnic in the park, and me and some of my mates are all getting a lift down to Leeds as soon as we get our envelopes.

BETTE. I never wanna see anyone from my school ever again TBH.

ALEX. Mood.

BETTE. What's in Leeds then?

ALEX. Leeds Fest... fancy it? It's about time we hung out IRL!

BETTE. Maybe...? Who's playing?

ALEX. Literally everyone... but most importantly...

   P A T R I C K W O L F.

BETTE. Oh no you didn't!

   You know I've always wanted to see Patrick Wolf live!

   ...But you also know I can't afford it.

ALEX. Here's the best part! So Joey got suspended for taking poppers into an exam so he isn't allowed to go any more!!!!

   He has to sell his ticket at half-price so... I got you first dibs!!!

BETTE. Oh wow – are you being serious?

ALEX. As serious as you are about these weird pets.

BETTE. Oi!

ALEX. We booked early so got last year's prices, a hundred and twenty-five pounds full price, so that's... sixty-two pounds fifty.

BETTE. I'll ask Mum.

ALEX. It's the full three days, four if you don't wanna collect your results in person! You can camp with us – Jimmy's dad is coming (and he grows his own).

BETTE. Yeah, I'll ask Mum.

ALEX. Or you can camp with other people, like if you don't want to be with the LADS LADS LADS all weekend...

I just thought...

We can party and hang out and see some epic bands. You can watch me go crazy in a moshpit and we can have like a conversation face to face!

BETTE. I'll ask Mum.

ALEX. I thought you'd be excited.

BETTE. I am excited?

It's just... a lot of stuff to figure out.

My brain hasn't got past my last exam yet TBH.

ALEX. You do wanna meet me, don't you?

BETTE. Of course I do idiot – it's just not that easy is it. I may have plenty of Neocash but I'm not sure Mountain Warehouse will accept that when I try to buy a tent...

ALEX. Worth a shot.

BETTE. I'll try to give it a go if you give Neopets a go too?

ALEX. You've got yourself a deal.

Scene Seven

BBM – 2006

BETTE. I mean, we're both gonna wanna be at the front for Patrick Wolf right? Even if that's the only time we see each other, could we meet there?

ALEX. I'm gonna be wasted and coated in mud most of the time, it's not like we're guaranteed to bump into each other.

BETTE. Wasted eh? Does this mean I'll be seeing you at your wild and raucous-est?

ALEX. Raucous-est? Ahaha I mean, maybe – you'll certainly be seeing me at my sweatiest?

BETTE. Three nights with no showers,
    I think we'll all be stanky bb.

ALEX. Try three days, no showers, the Foo
    Fighters moshpit AND a binder. I'm
    gonna S T I N K.

BETTE. Oh shit yeah – I hadn't even
    thought about that.

ALEX. Sweaty, and painful. I sneezed
    yesterday and you wouldn't believe the
    bruises on my ribs this morning! Are you
    sure you don't wanna camp with us?

BETTE. I told you – I promised Mum I'd
    camp with the Stevensons and their St
    John Ambulance nerds, it's the only way
    she's letting me go.

    And a bruise?! Is that normal? That
    doesn't sound safe?

ALEX. The Stevensons sound LAME!!!! Plz
    plz plz plz plz?

    I've been searching through forums
    online and it sounds like it's kinda
    standard for newbies, I did fuck up at
    first though, I was using duct tape.

BETTE. Fucking hell Al! How do you have
    any nips left?

ALEX. Well hopefully in a few years
    I won't?

BETTE. The nipless wonder king?

ALEX. I mean, maybe I'll get new nips? Or they'll reattach these bad boys – but I've been thinking a lot about gender presentation and what it actually means – like, blokes don't need nipples do we? And I wouldn't have any sensation left in them so it's not like it's worth keeping them for that... it would just be to look 'normal'.

BETTE. And what's normal anyway?

ALEX. Amen sister?

NOW STOP DISTRACTING ME LET'S MAKE A PROPER PLAN FFS.

BETTE. I've made a plan with the Stevensons?

ALEX. No... The Stevensons made a plan to live out their mediocre midlife crisis by volunteering at a music festival and are reluctantly letting you tag along because your mum's a control freak.

BETTE. She is not a...

ALEX. You got the ticket right?

BETTE. I sure did.

ALEX. Still dunno why you made me address it to your dad? And I thought your dad's name was like Paul or something?

BETTE. Lol no... dunno where you got that idea from.

ALEX. Paul and Carol, I swear that's what you said.

BETTE. Paul's not his actual first name, it's his middle name – it's what everyone calls him... because... he's tall! He's Tall Paul.

Beat.

ALEX. Lol okay.

Joey got the bank transfer too, so send thanks to your dad.

Beat.

I'm so hyped but... I don't know why I'm nervous.

BETTE. You're nervous?!

ALEX. I dunno – it feels like a big deal, dunnit? First time meeting IRL, first time meeting someone who actually knows me, first time hearing my name out loud.

BETTE. You don't need me for any of that.

ALEX. I do.

Scene Eight

2006

ALEX *is at Leeds Festival with his school friends, but* BETTE *hasn't been in touch. She said she'd text him when her tent was up and they'd find each other but...* BETTE *is too nervous. She still hasn't told* ALEX *that she's Trans, let alone that she's not out offline, so presents as male.*

ALEX *is texting* BETTE, *trying to reach her not knowing that she can actually see him – he just doesn't recognise her.*

Day One:

ALEX. Here! We're aiming for Red.

Red Camping that is – just realised we never talked about where to camp! Tell the Stevensons to camp in Red – it's the closest to the arena.

We've staked out a spot to the right of the taps and downwind of the bogs! Trying to save the spot next to us too so come quick?

Where are you I'm druuunnnkkkk.

Day Two:

Sorry about last night – my phone died and I was so drunk I couldn't stand up at the charging point, I dunno if you called me but hopefully you're in and settled now?

Just picked up if you fancy a smoke?

Scratch that.

It was literal dirt, from the ground.

Fucking twenty pounds too?

Idiot Al?

We're gonna grab a Yorkshire pudding wrap before heading into the arena, doing Lady Sov, Hot Chip, TBS, MCR and Placebo hopefully! Tb x.

How could you miss MCR?????

Did you miss MCR??

Where are you?

What have the Stevensons done with you??

Are you in some kind of kinky throuple with them now?!

Lol JK, but TEXT ME BACK.

Are these going through?

Just met Fightstar and made Charlie sign my Busted T-shirt.

Are you ignoring me?

B!!!!

This is just shitty now B, I got you the fucking ticket – you wouldn't be here if it wasn't for me!

Are you even here?

The lads think I made you up.

Just let me know you're safe?

Fuck you Bette.

Day Three:

Sorry – drunk again. Maybe today you'll respond?

Starting today with Aiden, then Coheed and Cambria 'n' Muse tonight if you wanna join.

Guess not.

Are you really gonna make me dance to Patrick Wolf on my own?

BETTE *types then deletes.*

It was beautiful. I cried. Some baby gay gave me a Barbie tissue.

BETTE *types and then deletes:*

BETTE. That was me.

Delete.

Day Four:

ALEX. Final chance – camping out at the mainstage today for Panic! Fall Out Boy and the Yeah Yeah Yeahs.

Bette I don't know what's going on with us but can you please put whatever it is aside for one minute 'cause I fucking need you right now.

ALEX *calls* BETTE *fifteen times – she doesn't pick up once.*

Nothing?

A week later:

What the actual fuck B? It's been a week? What's happened? Hello.

Hi.

Hey.

Bette?

Bette?

Scene Nine

MSN – 2006

ALEX. You're online.

BETTE. Yeah.

ALEX. What happened?

BETTE. I'm sorry.

I saw your results status – well done.

Beat.

ALEX. We coulda celebrated together.

BETTE. I know.

ALEX. How did you do?

BETTE. Sailing through to sixth form unfortunately.

ALEX. Just got swallowed up by the crowd I guess?

BETTE. Something like that.

ALEX. Oh come on.

Beat.

Why are you being like this?

BETTE. It's complicated.

ALEX. You're not Avril Lavigne.

I needed you.

BETTE. What happened?

ALEX. My best friend deserted me that's what happened.

BETTE. You had other friends there.

ALEX. That's not the point.

BETTE. Don't be like that.

ALEX. Don't be like what?

Don't have emotions?

Don't expect my friend to be there for me? Don't call her out on her bullshit?

You should have been there.

I had to go home.

I was a fucking mess.

BETTE. What happened?

BETTE *nudges* ALEX, *causing their chat screen to shake.*

ALEX. What happened was I packed like a boy, because I thought my BFF would be there to support my first weekend living 'in role' or whatever bullshit it's called now.

The lads didn't know anything obviously, they asked why my bra was so tight for fuck's sake.

It was a nightmare – I couldn't even bring myself to use the loos.

It was alright on day one when everyone was arriving – it was quiet, I could squat behind the tent but then...

BETTE. Then...?

ALEX. Then I called you, and you didn't answer. Fifteen times I called before I got the fucking hint and just called Dad to pick me up.

BETTE. You went all the way home just to use the loo?

ALEX. I went all the way home because I couldn't face the toilets and ended up shitting myself in front of all the lads while my supposed best friend was ignoring me!! And kept ignoring me for a fucking month!!

BETTE. I'm sorry.

ALEX. So you keep saying.

BETTE. I know but it's true.

How are your ribs doing?

ALEX. You don't get to just change the conversation.

Where were you?

Did you turn up and not like the look of me?

Was it all a joke all along?

Let's laugh at the weird Transgender and pretend we're mates?

Do you even exist?

BETTE. Does it matter if I exist?

ALEX. Of course it fucking matters??????????????????????????????

What are you even on about? Is that some kind of admission? Who are you really eh?

Actually, fuck this – I don't care who you are.

ALEX *blocks* BETTE.

BETTE. I really am sorry.

I was going to tell you... I'd planned this whole speech. You with a beer in hand, me with a WKD – sat on the grass.

I swear I wanted to tell you everything: about how you mistaking me for a girl felt good at first... about how it started to feel right. I was going to tell you how every time you used 'she/her' for me my heart would grow about four sizes.

But then you didn't recognise me... at all.

You've already logged out haven't you.

The one time you looked at me, you saw a 'baby gay', and I... I didn't want to be a baby. I certainly didn't want you thinking of me as a baby.

I wanted to be brave for you, brave like you but...

Oh what's the point – you'll never see this.

Scene Ten

Facebook – 2007

BETTE *is scrolling through Facebook, it's bleak. All 'Weston Supermare Spotted' and Buzzfeed listicles. She mutes a Transphobic meme, and we notice she's in multiple Trans femme Facebook groups.*

She scrolls through comments on her latest group post and they are all along the lines of 'you've got this', ' you can tell them' ,'we believe in you', etc.

Next she scrolls to her 'people you may know' and clicks through.

She finds ALEX*'s page and notices he's updated his name to* ALEC. *She scrolls through what she can see publicly but then decides to add him.*

He accepts.

She scrolls through posts for his last week at college and then his uni freshers' week, liking pictures of him at prom and on nights out, checking who else has liked them, etc.

She refreshes her notifications to see if ALEC *has gone to check her out simultaneously – but nothing appears.*

Scene Eleven

Hotmail and Facebook – 2008

BETTE *is sending* ALEC *an email,* ALEC *is replying – but he doesn't reply directly, he replies via a public Facebook status to all his friends, basically ignoring* BETTE. *The audience does not realise he isn't replying directly until the end of his post.*

BETTE. Hey Alex.

   Delete.

   Hey Alec.

   I know it's been a while... I wanted to check in.

   I saw on FB you're up in Newcastle now?

   Are you all settled into halls?

ALEC. Alec Copley is... doing fine thanks?

I know I've had about a million emails
and texts over the past few weeks.

BETTE. How's the new name sitting? How
is freshers' week? What are your new
flatmates like?

ALEC. Move-in day! Housemates seem
chill and I'm definitely gonna get my
five a day here (wine comes from
grapes, right?).

BETTE. I hope they're being better friends
to you than I was...

ALEC. Can you still get freshers' flu in
second year? To be honest I'm not
feeling this...

BETTE. I'm trying to be more honest with
people these days, especially people
I care about. And I do still care about
you. I came out – maybe not in the way
you were expecting but... I'm actually
Trans too!

ALEC. Oh god, I totally rinsed my student
card at Topman, so prepare to be
inundated with a million selfies of me
looking fly in my new printed shirts and
skinny jeans.

BETTE. You were so honest and open
about who you were from day dot –
I guess I was maybe intimidated by

that? This sounds like I'm blaming you –
which I'm not! Quite the opposite
actually – I know it's corny and gross
when Transfolk get called brave or
inspiring but I get it y'know?

You definitely are.

ALEC. Can't wait for tonight's screening of
Hedwig and the Angry Inch in D Block
Studio Three... apparently this movie
has nothing to do with a magic owl, and
a lot to do with being a Trans rockstar
so... that should be a fun insight into
my future!

BETTE. You always saw me as a girl and
I really liked that, but everyone else
knew me as a boy.

I had no idea how to get from who
everyone else saw me as to who you
saw me as and who I wanted to be.
I didn't have the vocabulary or the
fucking strength to tell my family let
alone you, and you really were the most
important person in my life back then.

ALEC. We've got the Queer Soc elections
coming up and I'm running for social
secretary so get your votes in now and
tell me what sort of events you want!

BETTE. Coming out to cis people – it
makes my insides feel like an empty

crisp packet, and each little step out the closet is yet another fold. Does that make sense? Like when old men at the pub fold crisp packets up into a perfect triangle, y'know?

Every word of truth just makes me smaller and smaller in their eyes... until eventually the table gets cleared away and they forget they even had crisps to begin with.

ALEC. When I pictured all-nighters at uni, they featured a lot more beer and a lot less books!

BETTE. I'm sorry I'm only just telling you this now, and it is not an excuse at all... but maybe it's an explanation? I hope in some way you might understand? You always managed to unfold me, to smooth out the creases.

I'm trying to learn to do it for myself.

ALEC. I'm working hard, not hard-working. I even got my first first for a practical assignment today!

BETTE. I did finally come out to my family and start my transition though, so now I get to be me IRL too.

And it's not just gender games! I gave myself a crash course in Python and

C++, and after computer camp I swapped from Windows XP for Linux... but that probably won't mean anything to you.

I'm such a fuckin' nerd.

ALEC. Internet is down on campus today so text me if you need me!

BETTE. I miss you, would you maybe want to Skype soon – do you have internet in your flat or do you have to go to the library?

ALEC. Alec Copley is... frantically trying to learn a new song before tomorrow's practical assessment #LastMinuteLad.

BETTE. I hope to hear from you soon, but if I don't I totally understand. I really am sorry Alec.

You know you love me, XOXO Gossip Girl.

Scene Twelve

Instagram – 2009

ALEC *is scrolling Instagram and a pop-up ad appears on his feed, it's an app called #SAFESHIT.* ALEC *clicks on the ad and sees that it's 'The UK's Number One Resource for Gender Neutral Bathrooms across the country'.*

ALEC *downloads the app.*

He logs in.

We see a map of the UK covered in pins denoting GN toilets. ALEC *gets an automated message from the app.*

BETTE. Hello and welcome to Hashtag SafeShit, a resource made by and for the Trans community. I'm Bette the founder and CEO, you can find many more resources on our website SafeShit.com and if you have any questions reply to this message and one of our team will get back to you shortly. Kthanksbye?

ALEC. Hi Bette.

BETTE. Thank you for messaging Hashtag SafeShit, I'm afraid I didn't understand your request. Please type your question clearly, or type asterisk to speak to our customer service team.

ALEC *closes the chat and goes back to Instagram, where he follows* BETTE *and sends her a text.*

Hi.

BETTE. Oh hey you.

ALEC. Long time.

BETTE. Indeed.

Beat.

ALEC. So I downloaded your app.

BETTE. It's still in beta.

ALEC. I think I know what inspired this.

BETTE. Always thought I'd end up being your muse, not the other way around...

Listen, I really am sorry – I emailed, but I guess I wanted to give you some space?

ALEC. I appreciate that – and I do miss you.

Scene Thirteen

Skype – 2011

BETTE *and* ALEC *are talking on Skype. We see their chat history but pick up halfway through their conversation.*

BETTE. Um... you have a boyfriend now!?!?!

ALEC. You mean Levi? Oh barely – we just hung out a couple of times!

BETTE. Since when did you like boys?

ALEC. I've never been a fan of gender in general TBH.

BETTE. It is a construct after all.

Proud of you.

ALEC. Ahahah shurrup.

BETTE. No seriously, boy done good.

ALEC. Ahaha he is cute right? But like I said... it's a nothing thing, we just make out when we're drunk lol.

BETTE. Ever the romantic.

ALEC. Oh I can be romantic.

BETTE. Can you now?

ALEC. Well if you don't ghost me again, maybe you'll find out...

BETTE. Is that a threat or a promise?

ALEC. Well Casper... Maybe I'll take you to a Patrick Wolf gig one day, and you can finally see him live.

BETTE. I've already seen him!

ALEC. You've seen him before!?!?

He understands.

Oh shit.

BETTE. Yeah, I was there.

ALEC. Oh babe.

BETTE. I was the baby gay.

You didn't recognise me.

I couldn't...

ALEC. Why didn't you tell me?

BETTE. I just...

ALEC. You really let me believe I was there all alone?

BETTE. You seemed alright with the lads... I came to find you to try and explain... but you were all setting up camp.

ALEC. You were watching us? That's a lil bit creepy, Bette – this isn't some rom com where we pretend stalking is a kind of romantic gesture lol.

BETTE. You were laughing with your friends, your life looked good, you'd already told me you were finally on the GIC waitlist and I guess I thought you were sorted?

ALEC. Babe, I'm a Sagittarius with a Twitter account, of course I look like I have it all together.

Social media isn't real, you know that right?

BETTE. I know I know.

ALEC. Simply existing takes work, time, effort, and emotional energy. The amount of gatekeeping I had to put up with, the amount of fucking hurdles I had to jump over because the NHS do not give a shit about Transpeople!

I've been waiting for top surgery for years and I'd still be waiting now if I relied on the GIC!

This did not just happen, I am making it happen. I found my hormones online, I've been self-medding for two years now, getting my bloods taken regularly – doing it all safely ofc and that, but still no GIC appointment!

I'm getting my top surgery next week because I did the research myself,

I trawled Reddit, I found a surgeon
I liked the look of, I checked their
results, I booked a flight to Poland, and
I worked two jobs in addition to uni so
I can pay for it myself!

BETTE. You never told me any of that.

ALEC. I didn't wanna worry you.

BETTE. Well I want to worry about you.
Please don't ever feel like you can't tell
me things... Maybe we're both on our
own journeys, but that doesn't mean
we're alone on them.

Maybe gender is like life? And like time
too? In that it doesn't actually exist,
and yet our world revolves around the
expectations we put on it.

We're always gonna be growing and
learning and finding out the new things
we need, together. I was born in exactly
the right body. You were born in exactly
the right body. These journeys we've
taken were the journeys we were meant
to take in order to find ourselves, and
maybe even each other?

ALEC. I wish I could hug you right now.

BETTE. Ditto.

Scene Fourteen

Club Penguin – 2012

We are back in the place where they first met, this time sitting outside the school bus. The website is noticeably glitchy, there are pop-ups for porn/Vlagra/'local women in your area', etc.

ALEC. I didn't even know this place still existed.

BETTE. It doesn't, technically.

ALEC. What do you mean?

BETTE. This is rewritten, I guess kinda like... a copy? Like a clone/rewrite of the OG on a public server – it's a bit messy but.

ALEC. Some people have too much time on their hands.

BETTE. I built it.

Beat.

ALEC. Oh shit, sorry, I didn't – I mean, FFS. Foot-in-mouth disease.

Long pause.

BETTE. It's okay – I know I'm a nerd. It wasn't just me of course – there are

probably thousands of users
contributing code and widgets and stuff.

ALEC. So... tell me about your rewrites
then?

BETTE. I started doing it again as I began
transitioning, I found the server and
built myself a little island to like...
practise I guess? I've always felt more
comfy online, it was never hard to make
friends or be myself here, so I guess it
was a safety net? Here I could go to the
'grocery store' or the ice rink as a
femme, and not feel watched.

Beat.

I could go to the places I felt I couldn't
go any more, until I worked up enough
courage to go IRL.

ALEC. So you hung out in an online bus?

BETTE. Pretty much, lol.

There were months when I hadn't left
my house... when I first started growing
my hair out and stuff, I started to miss
really basic things? Like buses! I mean,
even now I still catch myself feminising
my voice to buy a ticket! Here I don't
have to worry about all that, I know no
knobhead's gonna jump me or shout a
slur... I'm safe here.

ALEC. So where shall we sit?

BETTE. The top deck ofc.

ALEC. And which is your favourite seat?

BETTE. Who has a favourite seat?

ALEC. Okay a regular seat then, where have you been choosing to sit on your little busventures?

BETTE. I mean I guess I have a regular seat in the real world. Top deck, the first set of seats behind the stairs.

ALEC. Why?

BETTE. It's easier to sit with your knees up I guess, I like to slouch down.

Beat.

Make myself as small as possible.

ALEC. You're pretty big here.

BETTE. Oi.

ALEC. Not like that – you're just... the queen of the bus here.

BETTE. That's what I mean. It's a lot easier here – here I control who gets on and off the bus, where the bus goes, what it looks like – it's my damn bus?

Here I don't need to listen to my podcasts on loud, keeping an eye on who's coming up the stairs, I don't feel the need to have my keys in my fist at all times? I don't have to worry about accidentally catching the wrong person's eye and getting a broken nose.

ALEC. Oh babe.

BETTE. It's okay. It sounds worse than it is. I got used to it.

ALEC. I know.

And I know the looks I used to get, if someone spotted my binder, or my mascara mustache.

I know it's different though. Femmes get more attention.

Sometimes it's okay to blast some My Chemical Romance and lip-sync along to 'I'm Not Okay'.

BETTE. I was more of an 'Early Sunsets Over Monroeville' kinda gal, and we're not fifteen any more Al.

ALEC. Of course you were, you pretentious twat lol.

Beat.

Listen, what if we have our own seat on the bus? One that's just for us? It can be on the top deck, like you said; the first set of seats behind the stairs –

And when one of us sits there, we're sitting together, always.

You can sit by the window seat, and I'll take the aisle – guarding you from any knobheads who might come up.

This is our seat, and no one can take that away from us.

If I'm riding home after band practice, or on my way to uni devouring a Happy Meal, the rain making Newcastle a Technicolor blur, I'm gonna be leaving the seat next to the window and behind the stairs free. For you.

I sit on the aisle and leave my hand out if you need to hold it. Always.

BETTE. I'm holding it now.

ALEC. I know.

BETTE. Bit gay.

ALEC. Says you?

BETTE. Touché.

Scene Fifteen

Twitter, then REDDIT R/T4T – 2012

We scroll through Twitter with ALEC, *liking various pictures of Trans masc surgery results, retweeting memes and posts about NHS GIC wait times, until we see a tweet from a Reddit compilation account @RedditT4T with the screenname /r/T4T.*

ALEC *opens the page and reads* BETTE'*s post, at first it could be anyone's story...*

BETTE. r/T4T.

Subject Line: I dreamt about fucking my Trans best friend.

I finally admitted my crush on my [22 MTF] best friend [22 FTM].

Title: The Reunion.

It's not really a reunion when we've never met is it – but 'The Union' sounded a bit too American Civil War. After years of online banter and embarrassing attempts at flirting, I finally had the guts to meet my online best friend in real life for the first time.

I booked a cheap hotel near his flat and was expecting to be the only person to use it but... after a few rosé and lemonades we both ended up back at the hotel.

He seemed tentative, nervous even – but it worked. We fit together like puzzle pieces. We chose our own words for our junk, so that's what they were. It wasn't like playing pretend, it was the power of words and intentions.

He picked up my dysphoria like it was a teddy bear and cradled it until it fell asleep for a while.

I learnt to do the same for him. I knew what not to ask and what not to say. He looked so fucking hot, and you know what? I did too. Because Transpeople are fucking hot. And working this out felt like I'd unlocked some sort of magic portal... Our bodies intertwined just like our history, everything we'd said online and off for the past... however many years had led to this: To the best orgasm I'd ever experienced.

He was the first person to see my boobs. Like ever. He showed me his scar, making me trace my fingers along it... he can't feel his nipples yet – but I found this lil spot, just to the right of his scar, on the side of his torso and it drove him wild when I just softly kissed there.

The heteronormative sexual goal of climax just didn't exist for us? We enjoyed what we did and sometimes that led to climax, but sometimes it didn't and that was fine? It was a fucking joy.

Anyway, I guess I've been reading this sub for years so I thought I'd finally let myself indulge my own fantasies for y'all. But maybe I'll post again? Sorry it wasn't super detailed or explicit, but I'm sure if you go to the next post someone else will have written something lush you can have a wank over! I hope you enjoyed, or learnt something, or identified or whatever x.

Scene Sixteen

Facebook Messenger – 2012

ALEC *is about to finish uni. After his last night he chats with* BETTE *on Facebook.*

BETTE. How was the kegger?

ALEC. You watch way too many American movies.

BETTE. It's not my fault you never learnt about movies made after the nineteen eighties.

ALEC. I'll make a Jarman fan out of you yet.

BETTE. Did you dress up in the end or not?

ALEC. Kinda? I just did Joker facepaint and I just hoped it wasn't too reminiscent of make-up?

BETTE. The scariest halloween costume of them all: Dysphoria?

ALEC. I mean it was hard to get a Halloween costume in May so don't judge?

BETTE. Yeah, remind me what the fuck you were doing again?

ALEC. It's supposed to be the last gay Christmas before we all fuck off into adulthood. It's a Queer Soc tradition. You hand in your dissertation then go on a Halloween pub crawl... in May lol.

BETTE. How's the hangover.

ALEC. I've been better – I'm gonna get some food now.

BETTE. Where u off?

ALEC. McDonald's.

BETTE. Double large fries, and a flat Fanta?

ALEC. You know me well – and a Happy Meal for someone else.

Beat.

I can't believe it's done – no more uni, no more being separated by hundreds of miles.

BETTE. You think you'll move down south?!

ALEC. I think I'd be open to being persuaded...

BETTE. Ah so that's how this is going to work is it? I thought the boy made the first move...

ALEC. Oh wow – we're regressing to hetronormative gender stereotypes now are we? Next thing you'll be telling me all you wanna be is a housewife?

BETTE. You know what I mean.

Long pause.

Hold on a sec, I'm just getting on the bus.

ALEC. You gonna sit in our seats?

BETTE. I always do.

ALEC. Fancy holding my hand IRL this time?

BETTE. What d'ya mean?

We're on a bus, ALEC *is sat by the window with a Happy Meal for* BETTE. *We hear his iPhone playing Patrick Wolf through the headphones.*

ALEC. This seat's for you.

Their eyes meet, ALEC *removes his headphones as the music swells romantically. Rain hits the windows of the bus. There is tension, blackout.*

End of play.

www.nickhernbooks.co.uk

facebook.com/nickhernbooks

twitter.com/nickhernbooks